D1270419

How to Do Great Online Research

Kezia Endsley

Cavendish
Square
New York

To my dad, who inspired a lifelong love of learning. I love you.

Published in 2015 by Cavendish Square Publishing, LLC
243 5th Avenue, Suite 136, New York, NY 10016

Library of Congress Cataloging-in-Publication Data

Endsley, Kezia.
How to do great online research / by Kezia Endsley.
p. cm. — (Web wisdom)
Includes index.
ISBN 971-1-50260-193-3 (hardcover) ISBN 971-1-50260-192-6 (ebook)
1. Internet — Juvenile literature. 2. Computer network resources — Evaluation — Juvenile literature. 3. Web search engines — Juvenile literature. I. Endsley, Kezia, 1968-. II. Title.
ZA4201.E535 2015
025.04—d23

Editor: Andrew Coddington
Senior Copy Editor: Wendy A. Reynolds
Art Director: Jeffrey Talbot
Designer: Douglas Brooks
Senior Production Manager: Jennifer Ryder-Talbot
Production Editor: David McNamara
Photo Research: J8 Media

Printed in the United States of America

Contents

CHAPTER 1

A Blessing and a Curse!

In today's interconnected world, you have tons of data at your fingertips. With a few keystrokes or finger swipes, you can find out anything you're wondering about in a matter of seconds. Long gone are the days of tromping off to the local library to use that year's set of *Encyclopedia Britannica* books to look up the "latest" information about the government of Congo, for example. Ask your parents; they might remember those days.

Not only was information harder to access in printed books, it could become dated and stale as soon as the ink was dry! If you need to find out the latest news coming out of the Congo now, you can find literally minute-to-minute updates on the Internet.

In large part, this is great news for all of us with reliable Internet access. When it comes to researching a topic for a paper or report, we certainly do live in a golden age. However, Internet research is not without its drawbacks.

The printed resources found in libraries have almost always been thoroughly evaluated by experts before they are published. Also, when books and other materials come into the library system, they are catalogued and cross-referenced using procedures followed by research libraries the world over. This process is the basis for the way materials are organized in the library, and make the various search functions of the catalog possible. However, it can be difficult to find solid, reliable information on the Internet because *anyone* can post there, from respected experts to people who know nothing about a subject. When using the Internet, how do you locate research you can trust?

The challenge in doing online research well is basically four-fold:

- You need to know where and how to search efficiently to find the best information for your purposes.

- You need to be able to sort through the volumes of information and determine which sources are reliable and backed up with solid data and facts.

- You need to properly and ethically give credit where credit is due, which includes properly determining who has rights to the information.

- You need to always protect yourself when you're out on the web.

Searching Effectively

It all starts with the search. If your teacher or instructor does not give you some guidelines, you may be wondering how to best search for your category. Maybe you think it doesn't really matter, that you can just type a few words and away you go. The truth is, you will get much better and more specific results if you narrow your research topic down before you begin searching. The Internet allows access to so much information that you can easily be overwhelmed. Before you start your search, think about what you're looking for, and if possible come up with some very specific questions to direct and limit your search.

Google.com is good place to start any search.

For example, if you were writing a report about Amelia Earhart, you should ask yourself on what aspects of her life your report will focus. Then, write down questions related to your focus, whether it be her early life and childhood, her schooling, her fight against stereotypes, how she discovered her love of flying, her non-traditional marriage, the controversy surrounding her disappearance, recent developments in finding her plane, and so on. There are many different approaches you can take to writing about any subject, so it's better to do the work of narrowing your topic early and avoid browsing through millions of unrelated search results.

A quick Google search will provide multiple sources, but many of them might not be related to your specific topic.

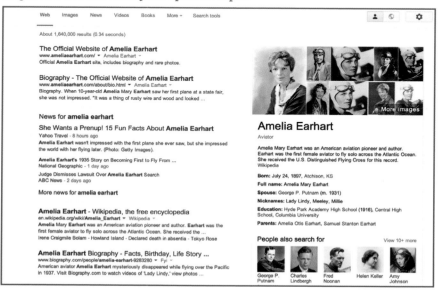

Finding reliable sources that are backed up with accurate, well-researched data can be a challenge, but you can tip the odds in your favor by using **search engines** that have already done the work of collecting reliable data for you. The added bonus is that they have also filtered out the inappropriate information as well. There are many topic-specific search engines out there that can serve you better than Google's one-site-fits-all approach. Tried-and-true websites such as *infomine. ucr.edu* and *education.iseek.com* are recommended and used by teachers and educators around the world. Of course, if your teacher tells you to use a specific site/sites, you should start there.

As part of choosing and using reliable sites, it's important that you keep a detailed record of sites you visit and use. Doing research on the web inevitably means visiting some sites that are useful, and many that are not. Keeping track is necessary so that you can revisit the useful ones later, and also put the required references in your paper. Don't just rely on your browser's History function, because it saves the web addresses, or **URLs**, of all the sites you visit—good or bad. By the time you're ready to go back to them, you might not remember which is which. Also, if you're using a computer at school, the library, or any public place, the memory in the

History file will be erased at the end of your session. It's better to write down or **bookmark** the sites you've found useful, so that you'll have a permanent record.

Properly Crediting Your Sources

It is very important to give credit to the creators of any articles, quotes, images, videos, music, charts, and so on, that you use in your reports. Not doing so is called **plagiarism**. It is the wrongful use of another person's ideas or creations without crediting them or, in some cases, getting permission to use their work. In addition to being unethical and illegal, it could very well earn you an F on a paper and perhaps some other punishment.

In later chapters, you'll learn about the Creative Commons license, which enables you not only to legally use and credit other authors' works, but also allows you to protect your own works that you create online. The Creative Commons license explains exactly how to credit other people's works to protect yourself and give credit where credit is due.

Most teachers suggest that students record their sources of information using *The Chicago Manual of Style* or the MLA (Modern Language Association) guidelines. The systematic process of recording your sources is called **citing** (pronounced "sighting") your source. You'll learn more about how

Be sure to keep track of your sources and properly credit them. Not doing so may land you in serious academic trouble.

to properly cite sources in the upcoming chapters. *The Chicago Manual of Style* has a website where you can get a quick look at properly citing your sources, check out chicagomanualofstyle.org/tools_citationguide.html. You can find the latest hardcopy editions of both of these guides (*The MLA Style Manual* and *The Chicago Manual of Style*) at your school or local library.

Being Safe, Anonymous, and Courteous

Any time you're on the web, whether you're searching for information, blogging and chatting, or even making purchases online, staying safe should be at the top of your mind. Keep yourself as anonymous as possible, and never give out your personal information. Most credible companies and sites will not ask you for personal information online. If one does, it should be a red flag to you that something might be amiss. If you ever feel uncomfortable or unsure on a site, leave it and tell a parent or adult right away so they can report the issue. If you are asked to create a login or screen name, use something with numbers and letters that doesn't identify you as male or female.

In terms of Internet research, being safe mostly means avoiding inappropriate and offensive websites as you're searching. One misguided search

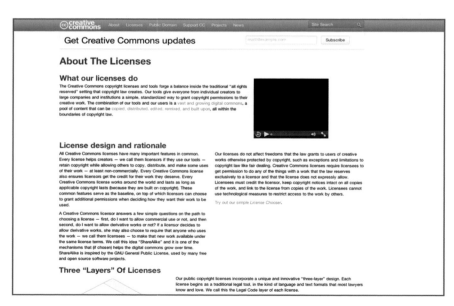

Visit creativecommons.org to find out how to search for and create material that you can reuse legally.

ONLINE NETIQUETTE

If during your research you do need to reach out to others online, such as the authors of articles and **blogs**, always be kind, honest, and clear in your message. Use proper grammar and correct spelling, and be calm in your approach. Respectfully interacting with others online is called good **netiquette**. Good netiquette involves respecting others' privacy and not doing anything online that would annoy or frustrate other people. Three areas where good netiquette is especially important are email, social media, and online chat. Don't type in all caps, for example, as this is interpreted online as yelling. Also, don't demand responses from the people you contact. Respectfully request a follow-up. If you are always calm, honest, and clear in your communications, you'll be covered.

Remember that you are communicating with real people who have feelings, even though you may never see or meet them. Another important part of being a good online citizen is giving proper credit to all your sources. You'll learn more about how to do that shortly.

on Google can land you somewhere you really don't want to be, including sites that can infect your computer with viruses. The best ways to avoid such sites is to search reliable, educational sites and to carefully choose your **keywords** before you search. If you've never searched the Internet before, it's a good idea to sit down with a parent or teacher and go through the process with someone who knows the dangers.

If you're using school computers, they probably have **Internet-filtering software** installed that filters out inappropriate websites. Ask your parents to look into such programs for your protection. If

Be selective when searching and ask for help from an adult when you get stuck.

all else fails, stay on sites that are well-known and reputable. You'll learn about many great sites in this book that you can use.

If you ever need to contact someone on the Internet during your research, such as an author of an article for a follow-up question, you should first get permission and guidance from a trusted adult. There should rarely be a reason that you'll need to contact someone when doing research for a paper or report.

Where Should You Start?

There is one important aspect of writing a research paper that hasn't changed in the years since your parents read through encyclopedias in the library for information. It all begins with a clear, specific, and well-thought-out idea. The clearer and more defined your research topic is, the better your search results will be, and it all rolls downhill from there. Before you lay one finger on a keyboard, make sure you have developed a well-defined topic that is interesting and relevant and can sustain a discussion length matching the number of words you need to write. Knowing what you want to find is the key to unlocking all of the knowledge on the web you need.

Getting Started on Your Research

In this chapter, we'll cover two main aspects of great searching, which are how to search and what to search. You'll learn:

- What kinds of sites will give you the best, most reliable results

- How to word your searches for best results

- How to verify whether or not a source is reliable

Searching for Maximum Results

The first step in getting reliable search results is to choose which types of websites are best for your research topic. Factual, non-opinion research topics require hard facts and respected evidence. An example of this kind of topic might be "The U.S. Bald Eagle Population Since 1972." An opinion blog is not an acceptable source here. Instead, you need to find publications by scholars, experts, and professionals with credentials. You'll want to start with academic journals, online encyclopedias, government publications, and/or scientific and medical content, all approved or written by known authorities.

Opinion papers are often about validating your opinion using the arguments of respected online writers. For example, "Why President Lincoln Was the Best President" might be an opinion piece topic. You can find resources for backing/validating your opinion in such places as personal blogs, forums and discussion sites, consumer product review sites, and technology and computer sites.

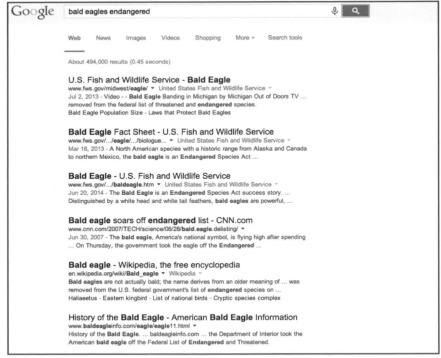

Narrowing your search with a topic word or phrase, such as "bald eagles endangered," will go a long way toward collecting sources that are actually useful.

Once you have an idea what kinds of sources or sites you need, you're ready to search. For best results, use different search engines and several three-to-five-word keyword combinations. Be patient, and don't be afraid to adjust your keywords as you learn more. Your searches should start broad and be narrowed down as you go.

For example, if you were writing a report on the increase in numbers of bald eagles as a result of their being protected by the U.S. government, you would first want to determine what kinds of sites provide the most reliable and up-to-date information. Then, come up with a few keyword searches to start your search. Keyword searches for your bald eagle report could include:

- Bald eagles endangered

- Bald eagle population

- Bald eagles DDT (an insecticide known to harm bald eagles)

- Bald eagles endangered list

- Bald eagles delisted

If you do a search for "bald eagles endangered," for example, you may see results returned from the U.S. Fish & Wildlife Service, Wikipedia, a site called baldeagleinfo.com, and an article from CNN.com from June 30, 2007, which is the day they were removed from the endangered list. The wisest step is to start with the U.S. Fish & Wildlife Service **link**. It is a U.S. government agency that's tasked with tracking wildlife and run by experts in fish and wildlife issues. You should bookmark the CNN.com article and read it later as well. What about baldeagleinfo.com? Well, you should use the critical skills you'll learn in the next section to decide whether this site is run by experts. Can you find information about the authors of the site? If not, use the U.S. Fish & Wildlife Service site instead.

Finally, go ahead and visit that Wikipedia page. You can use the "References" section at the bottom of each article as a jumping-off point for lots of other potential sources. However, never use that information as your only resource if you can't verify it elsewhere at a reputable site. Always use the original article, not Wikipedia, as your source.

Be sure to keep a list of the websites you're planning on using, and save them as bookmarks in your browser to stockpile all of this possibly useful content. While this step is simple, it is the second-slowest part of the whole process: gathering all the possible ingredients into organized piles that you can sift through later.

Verifying and Qualifying Your Sources

The slowest step of all is also the most important: filtering and validating the content you've collected. You've done some good, targeted searching and now have a lot of great information that you want to use in your report. However, before you quote or cite any of it, you need to research the truthfulness of that information. Start by answering these questions.

Who is the author of the information/site/ quote/etc.? Is the author's name given? Are her qualifications listed? Is there a link to more information about the author and her position? Has she written elsewhere on this topic, or have you heard of her before? Your job is to verify that this author actually exists and has the authority to write on this topic.

What is the website's affiliation? In other words, who sponsors the website? Does the information reflect the views of the organization, or only of the author? Would the organization and/or author have any interest in conveying biased information about this subject? If the sponsoring organization is not clearly identified on the site, check the URL. It may contain the name of a university or the domain **extension** ".edu," which is used by many educational institutions. Government sites are identified by the

References

SHOULD YOU USE WIKIPEDIA?

Nearly everyone has heard of wikipedia.org. Here's one hard-and-fast rule: never cite Wikipedia as a source. Wikipedia isn't an expert on a subject; it's the provider of secondary material written by others. That means you can use it as a jumping-off point to find expert sources you can use. Scroll down to the bottom of the Wikipedia page, to the "References" section, and start clicking those footnote links.

In the best-case scenario, a Wikipedia author has gathered information on your topic in one place, fully citing all sources at the bottom of the page. If you find a citation leading to a story from the *New York Times* about your topic, you need to go to that the *New York Times* archived site and read the story for yourself. Assuming this information is helpful and relevant, the *New York Times* becomes your source. In this way, Wikipedia can provide a quicker and easier way to find relevant and reliable sources on your topic.

In the worst-case scenario, the Wikipedia author has no sources, or inaccurate ones, or perhaps has a hidden agenda for writing this article. If you use the analytical methods described in this section for verifying a source, this will quickly become clear to you and you'll know not to use that information. If there is no secondary source listed on Wikipedia, don't use that information.

The bottom line is that you can use Wikipedia as a jumping-off point, as long as you critically analyze and verify the sources as you would any site, and as long as you never cite Wikipedia as your source.

extension ".gov." URLs containing ".org" are trickier and require research; these are sites sponsored by non-profit organizations, some of which are reliable sources and some of which are very biased. Sites with the ".com" extension should also be used with caution, because they have commercial or corporate sponsors who probably want to sell you something.

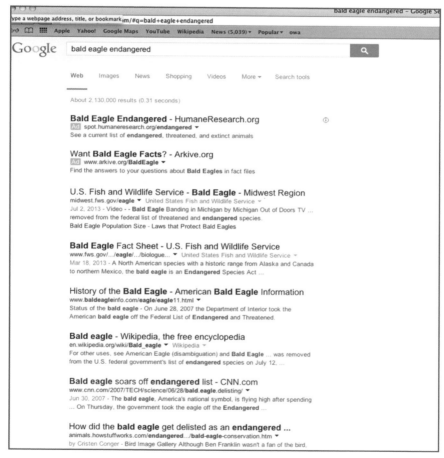

Pay attention to website domain extensions, such as .edu, .org, .gov, or .com, when searching. It's a quick and easy way to judge whether or not a site is credible.

What is the intended audience level of the website? Don't use sites that are too technical for your needs. For example, if you're in the sixth grade, you probably want to find information at the middle school and possibly high school level. A site intended for university students might be too advanced for your needs.

Is the website dated, or has it been updated recently? Is the information current? Look for a date when the site was last updated (usually found in the footer at the bottom of the page) and check to ensure that all the links on the site work. Broken links can mean the site is out of date; at the very least, they are a sign that it's not well maintained.

Is the site accurate and reliable? Is the information factual or opinion? Can you verify the information in print sources? Is the source of the information clearly stated, whether it's original research material or secondary material borrowed from elsewhere? Is the author's point of view impartial? Is the author's language free of emotion and bias? Are additional electronic and print sources provided to support the material?

If you can answer all these questions positively when looking at a particular site, you can be pretty sure it's a good one. If it doesn't measure up one way or another, it's probably a site to avoid. The key to the whole process is to think critically about what you find on the Internet. If you want to use it, you are responsible for ensuring that it is reliable and accurate.

Increasing Your Odds of Success

That's a lot of information to absorb. Let's take a minute to remember the main points here. Make the following points your mantra when doing your online research:

- Use the best, most accurate, and applicable sites for searching.

- Make sure your sources are reliable, accurate, and current.

- Be safe. Don't give out personal information, and stay with reputable sites!

- Cite all your sources fully and appropriately.

If you can keep these main points in mind as you research your topic, you're sure to be successful.

CHAPTER 3

Fine-Tuning the
Research Process

You've already learned how to search for best results, and how to check and verify your resources as reliable. This chapter covers some great places to start where you know the information is factual, reliable, and written by experts. You'll learn about academic-focused databases and websites that return results only from reliable sources. You'll also learn how to cite your sources (primary and secondary) and provide credit where credit is due.

Using Reliable Alternatives to Google and Bing

This section outlines many reliable sites that can be great resources for you. To begin, start with a broad initial search from these sites:

- Library-type sites such as **libraryspot.com** and **ipl.org** are great all-around spots to start research. Teachers use and recommend these sites. You can search by subject and age/grade, through newspaper and magazine archives, and even use Library Spot as a gateway to other safe and reliable sites.

- Check out **factmonster.com**, which defines itself as an online almanac, dictionary, encyclopedia, and homework helper. It's maintained by Pearson Education and even has a helpful section on how to cite articles you find there.

- Websites like **infomine.ucr.edu** and **education.iseek.com** are tried and true, and teachers use and recommend these sites. They both provide easy-to-use and helpful searching features to find your topics quickly.

- For learning videos organized by topic, check out **sqooltube.com** and Nova's video programs at **pbs.org/wgbh/nova/programs.html**. When you have

Watching online videos, such as those from Nova.com, are a great, fun way to learn about a topic.

information from Nova, for example, you can rest assured that it's accurate and timely.

- For an online dictionary, check out **dictionary.com**, and for an online thesaurus, check out **thesaurus.com**.

Is your topic confined to American geography or history? If so, you have the entire U.S. government's massive collection of websites at your disposal. Many government-related sites contain lots of good information from experts. Try these:

THE CREATIVE COMMONS LICENSE

You no doubt understand by now how important it is to credit the creator of the original work that you reuse or repurpose for your own reports. Many people create content for the purpose of sharing it on the Internet, but that doesn't mean you can use it without crediting them. One way that people protect their intellectual property on the Internet is by using a Creative Common license. These licenses "provide a simple, standardized way to give the public permission to share and use creative work—on conditions of [their] choice."

In fact, you can use a Creative Commons license to protect your own original creations if you were to post them on the Internet. Visit *creativecommons.org* to find out how to use a license on your own material, as well as to search for material that you can reuse legally. You can search the site for article, images, and more. All you have to do is cite the licensing and credit information provided.

- The **kids.usa.gov** site calls itself "a safe place to learn and play." Topics are organized by subject and grade level, and the searching capability is helpful and responsive.

- The U.S. Library of Congress site has a specific area for kids and families at **www.loc.gov/families**. This site contains lots of links about American history and culture, a performing arts encyclopedia, a "today in history" link, a collection of famous U.S. prints and photographs, and a veterans' history project, where you can listen to eyewitness accounts from American veterans of many wars.

- For all things space, be sure to check out NASA's student-geared site at **nasa.gov/audience/forstudents**. You can organize the site by grade level and then search by subject. It contains lots of video explanations and illustrations of math and science topics related to flight, such as aerodynamics and robotics.

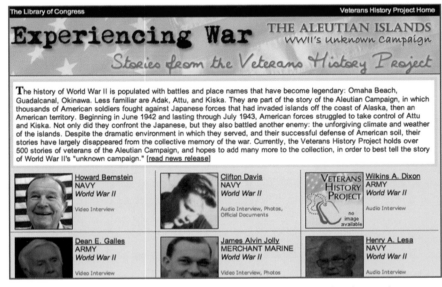

For information about American history and culture, check out the Library of Congress website.

- Doing a report on the effect of the national speed limit? Check out the National Highway Traffic Safety Administration at **nhtsa.gov** for lots of safety data. Writing a paper on some issue related to conservation? Check out the U.S. Fish & Wildlife Service website at **fws.gov**. Need information about the U.S. population, including how it's growing and where? Check out the U.S. Census Bureau at **census.gov**.

- For a complete list of the U.S. government's departments and agencies, go to **usa.gov/directory/federal/index. shtml**. You can simply click the links and be taken to the site that's related to your research topic.

Citing Made Easy (Well ... Easier?)

The first step to proper citing is to verify which format your teacher wants you to use. The two most widely used formats come from *The Chicago Manual of Style* and the MLA (Modern Language Association). If your teacher doesn't provide you with specific guidelines, pick one method and use it consistently across the board. Sources should follow alphabetical order.

Also, make sure you determine whether you are dealing with a **primary source**, which means an author actually witnessed the event, or a secondary source. A secondary source that is reporting on other primary sources should have citations to the primary sources it used as information.

Here are the general rules to follow:

- For online articles, the format is: Author's Last Name, Author's First Name. "Title of Web Page." Online. Retrieved Month Day, Year from <complete URL>.

Example: Smith, Matt. "Searchers unearth grave of "E.T.," the video game Atari wanted us to forget." Online. Retrieved May 23, 2014 from <www.cnn.com/2014/04/27/tech/gaming-gadgets/atari-et-video-game/>

- For citing a general website with no listed author, the format is: "Article Title." Website Title. Publisher of Website. Retrieved Month Day, Year article from <URL>

Example: "We want to leave the world better than we found it." Apple's Environmental Responsibility. Apple Inc. Retrieved May 12, 2012 from <www.apple.com/environment/>

- To reference sub-articles of a large reference site, such as an online encyclopedia: Author's Last Name, Author's First Name. "Subject/Article Title." *Encyclopedia/Reference Name Online*. Retrieved Month Day, Year from <URL>

Example: Randolph, John. "Water Pollution." *Grolier Multimedia Encyclopedia*. Grolier Online. Retrieved April 5, 2014 from <gme.grolier.com/cgi-bin/article?assetid=0231955-0>

There can be variations to these general guidelines, but if you are consistent, you will be able to easily cite all of your sources. You should remember, though, to always cite the original creator of the information, not a secondary source. It's your job to determine who created the information. If you can't determine the original author, don't use that information. Also, if an author is listed for the online article, blog, periodical, etc., be sure to always include that information. When no author is listed, listing the website, blog, or publisher is sufficient. Lastly, be sure to include the date when you last referenced the website. Things change quickly on the Internet, and providing a date helps to prove that the information you accessed is accurate.

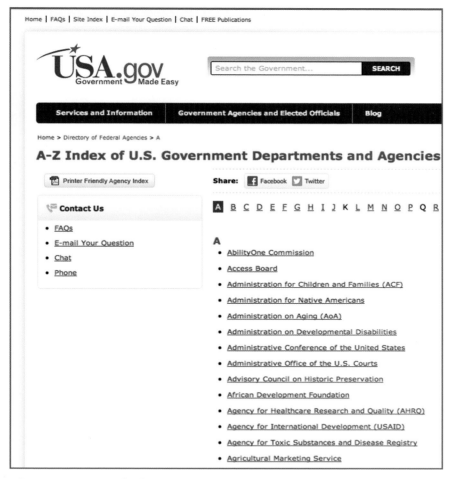

If you aren't sure which governmental agency has the information you need, start at USA.gov.

CHAPTER 4

Online Research Example

If you feel like you understand the theory behind great online research, but don't yet have a real grasp of how it all translates, don't worry! This chapter provides a specific example to help show how you can use search results to write effectively and intelligently on a topic. It also provides some tips and tricks for getting the most out of your Google searches.

Researching an Opinion Piece

Writing a good opinion paper, as mentioned in Chapter Two, involves finding respected and well-thought-out sources that back up and validate your opinion. Before you explain your point of view and use other sources to back up your argument, however, you need to investigate and understand the facts surrounding your topic.

The best way to start off is to search for basic facts about your topic. As an example, let's say you're writing about the minimum wage—the lowest rate of pay for an hour of work in the United States. Your search might start with simple questions: What is the current minimum wage? When was it established? When was it last raised? Have certain states raised their wages beyond the national rate, and how have those areas been affected?

To begin, you should determine what "minimum wage" means in this context. You can start simply enough by typing "define: minimum wage" into a Google search box. You'll see the result, "the lowest wage permitted by law or by a special agreement (such as one with a labor union)," along with other links to more detailed definitions.

Wage and Hour Division (WHD)

CHANGES IN BASIC MINIMUM WAGES IN NON-FARM EMPLOYMENT UNDER STATE LAW: SELECTED YEARS 1968 TO 2013

State or other jurisdiction	1968 (a)	1970 (a)	1972	1976 (a)	1979	1980	1981
Federal (FLSA)	$1.15 & $1.60	$1.30 & $1.60	$1.60	$2.20 & $2.30	$2.90	$3.10	$3.35
Alabama	-	-	-	-	-	-	-
Alaska	2.10	2.10	2.10	2.80	3.40	3.60	3.85
Arizona	18.72 - 26.40/wk(b)	18.72 - 26.40/wk(b)	18.72-26.40/wk(b)	...			
Arkansas	1.25/day(b)	1.10	1.20	1.90	2.30	2.55	2.70
California	1.65(b)	1.65(b)	1.65(b)	2.00	2.90	2.90	3.35
Colorado	1.00 - 1.25(b)	1.00 - 1.25(b)	1.00 - 1.25(b)	1.00 - 1.25(b)	1.90	1.90	1.90
Connecticut	1.40	1.60	1.85	2.21 & 2.31	2.91	3.12	3.37
Delaware	1.25	1.25	1.60	2.00	2.00	2.00	2.00
Florida	-	-	-	-	-	-	-
Georgia	-	-	1.25	1.25	1.25	1.25	1.25
Hawaii	1.25	1.60	1.60	2.40	2.65	2.90	3.10
Idaho	1.15	1.25	1.40	1.60	2.30	2.30	2.30
Illinois	-	-	1.40	2.10	2.30	2.30	2.30
Indiana	1.15	1.25	1.25	1.25	2.00	2.00	2.00
Iowa	-	-	-	-	-	-	-
Kansas	-	-	-	-	1.60	1.60	1.60
Kentucky	.65 - .75(b)	.65 - .75(b)	.65 - .75(b)	1.60	2.00	2.15	2.15
Louisiana	-	-	-	-	-	-	-
Maine	1.40	1.60	1.40 - 1.80	2.30	2.90	3.10	3.35
Maryland	1.00 & 1.15	1.30	1.60	2.20 & 2.30	2.90	3.10	3.35
Massachusetts	1.60	1.60	1.75	2.10	2.90	3.10	3.35
Michigan	1.25	1.25	1.60	2.20	2.90	3.10	3.35
Minnesota	.70 - 1.15(b)	.70 - 1.15(b)	.75 - 1.60	1.80	2.30	2.90	3.10
Mississippi	-	-	-	-	-	-	-
Missouri	-	-	-	-	-	-	-
Montana	-	-	1.60	1.80	2.00	2.00	2.00
Nebraska	1.00	1.00	1.00	1.60	1.60	1.60	1.60
Nevada	1.25	1.30	1.60	2.20 & 2.30	2.75	2.75	2.75
New Hampshire	1.40	1.45 & 1.60	1.60	2.20 - 2.30	2.90	3.10	3.35
New Jersey	1.40	1.50	1.50	2.20	2.50	3.10	3.35
New Mexico	1.15 - 1.40	1.30 - 1.60	1.30 - 1.60	2.00	2.30	2.65	2.90
State or other							

Even when writing an opinion piece, you still need hard facts, such as statistics, to back it up.

Next, if you search for "minimum wage," you'll discover that the governmental body responsible for it is the Department of Labor. Their site (*dol.gov*) contains lots of factual information about the minimum wage, including a clickable U.S. map that charts the wage in each state and a historical table that charts the changes to the minimum wage in each state since 1968. This is a great place to get your bearings and understand the facts before you research and craft your opinion. You can trust the U.S. government site to provide factual information about the minimum wage.

In general, you can find resources for backing up, or validating, your opinion at such places as personal blogs, forums and discussion sites, consumer product review sites, and online newspaper and magazine sites. In all these cases, however, you need to ensure that the article is written by a credible source. It's also important to try to determine that person's agenda or personal or political stance if they have one.

Is the author's name given, are her qualifications listed, and is there a link to more information about the author and her position? Has she written elsewhere on this topic, or have you heard of her before? Your job is to verify that this author actually exists and has the authority to write on this topic. Also, who sponsors the website? Would the organization and/or author have any interest in conveying biased information about this subject? If the sponsoring organization is not clearly identified on the site, check the URL closely for more information.

As an example, if you search for "increasing the minimum wage pros and cons," you'll get opinions from a wide variety of sources. Three examples are a *salary.com* article written by a freelance journalist, an article from the *Chicago Tribune* by a long-time contributor to that newspaper, and an article from a site called *whenIwork.com*, which is also authored by a long-time writer. In all three cases, the author's bio is available and you can click on their names to find out more about their credentials.

Try to read and consider at least three different opinions from credible and non-biased sources before you build your case. In the case of the pros and cons for raising the minimum wage, there are many sources/articles available, so you can draw from even more sources to develop and build your argument.

Writing a Well-Researched Paper

You should now understand what it takes to find accurate and compelling information online that will lead to your best paper yet. When you start with compelling search terms and you search sites that you know are reliable, you'll be much more likely to find the information you need to write a strong, interesting, and factual paper. Be sure to cite all your sources and always remember to be safe, anonymous, and courteous online.

You're ready to research and write your best research paper ever!

GOOGLE TIPS AND TRICKS

Google offers lots of ways you can use the search function to get better information more quickly. Try to incorporate some of these tips and tricks into your everyday searching techniques:

- Typing "define term" gives the definition of that term. For example, you would type "define autocratic" in the search window to get the definition of the word "autocratic."

- The "site: operator" is helpful in many ways. It's basically a filter that helps you narrow the search results so that Google doesn't have to. For example, if you want to know about Ireland but you only want to know what CNN has to say about it, you can perform this query:

ireland site:cnn.com <cnn.com>

This will limit the search results only to cnn.com.

- You can use also the site: operator as a negative filter, eliminating one or more sites from the search results. For example, if you want to know about Kanye West but don't want to hear what TMZ.com or Wikipedia say about him, you can use this search:

kanye west -site:tmz.com <tmz.com> -site:wikipedia.org <wikipedia.org>

Using the minus sign before the "site:" search tells the search engine to leave out results from those sites.

- The site: operator also narrows the results down to a type of site. For example, if you want to show only government results about how to start a business, this query limits results to only ".gov" sites:

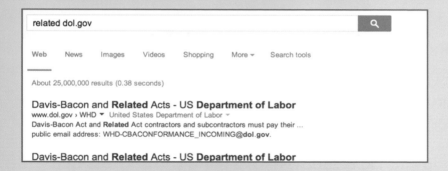

how to start a business site:.gov

Note that there is no space between the colon and the next character when using the site: operator.

- The "related: operator" shows sites that are similar to a site you enter in your query. For example, to find sites similar to the NFL, use the following query:

related:nfl.com <nfl.com>

- The minus sign also helps filter queries by concept. If you are looking for information about falcons (the bird), you don't want to get search results that contain information about the Atlanta Falcons. Use the following query to filter out information about the football team:

falcons -football

- The double-period serves as a "span" operator, returning results in a range. For example, to find out who the U.S. president(s) were during the time period 1958–1962, use this query:

us president 1958..1962

Of course, Bing and other sites have their own tricks and techniques, and if you prefer a different search engine, visit their sites to find out more.

GLOSSARY

blog Personal websites that users create to record and share frequent (often daily) opinions, musings, stories/poems, links, and more. Companies, organizations, groups, and other affiliations also have blogs centered on their purpose and activities.

bookmark A method for saving the address of a web page so that you can easily find it again. You add a bookmark through your browser's menu command when you are at the site you want to bookmark. Also called a favorite.

cite The systematic process of recording and crediting your sources of information in a report or project.

extension The part of the file name that comes after the dot and indicates to people and computers what kind of data is stored in that file (such as .doc for Microsoft Word word processing files). Likewise, a *domain extension*, such as .gov for governmental sites, is the last part of a web address after the dot and indicates what kind of website it is.

Internet-filtering software Software installed on a computer or network that blocks unwanted and inappropriate content and provides a safe Internet experience.

keywords "Key" terms and phrases that are used to search online sites and web search engines such as Google.

link In Internet language, a reference to another document. These are sometimes called hot links because they take you to another document when you click on them.

netiquette The correct or acceptable way of communicating on the Internet. Good netiquette involves respecting others' privacy and not doing anything online that would annoy or frustrate other people.

plagiarism The wrongful use of another person's ideas or creations without crediting them or, in some cases, getting permission to use their work.

primary source A document or physical object that was written or created during the time under study, including original documents such as diaries, speeches, manuscripts, letters, interviews, news film footage, autobiographies, and official records.

search engine A computer program that people use to find information on the Internet.

URL (uniform resource locator) The technical term for the website address.

FIND OUT MORE

The following books and websites will take you to the next step in your online research.

Books

Musgrave, Jim. *Online Research Made Easy*. San Diego, CA: Contemporary Instructional Concepts Publishers, 2012.

Rozakis, Laurie. *The Complete Idiot's Guide to Research Methods*. New York, NY: Penguin Group (USA) Inc., 2004.

Schneider, Fritz, Nancy Blachman, and Eric Fredricksen. *How to Do Everything with Google*. Emeryville, CA: McGraw-Hill Osborne, 2012.

Websites

The Chicago Manual of Style Online
www.chicagomanualofstyle.org

This online version of the manual is completely searchable and provides recommendations on editorial style and publishing practices for the digital age. You can use it to learn how to properly cite your references.

Kids.Gov
kids.usa.gov

The U.S. government's official web portal for kids. Topics are organized by subject and grade level and the searching capability is helpful and responsive.

Library Spot
www.libraryspot.com

This is a great all-around teacher-recommended research repository. You can search by subject, by age/grade, through newspaper and magazine archives, and even use it as a gateway to other safe and reliable sites.

Purdue University Owl: Online Writing Lab
owl.english.purdue.edu/owl/section/1/2/

Purdue University's Online Writing Lab is a fantastic resource for students who don't know where to begin an essay or need some tips on finer touches. This site links to helpful articles on everything ranging from establishing an argument to structuring a sentence.

BIBLIOGRAPHY

Calishain, Tara & Rael Dornfest. *Google Hacks, 100 Industrial-Strength Tips & Tools.* Sebastopol, CA: O'Reilly & Associates, Inc. 2009.

Cornell University Digital Literacy Resource. "A Guide to Online Research." Accessed May 29, 2014 from http://digitalliteracy.cornell.edu/tutorial/dpl3000.html.

Gil, Paul. "How Proper Online Research Works." About.Com/Internet for Beginners, June 2014. http://netforbeginners.about.com/od/navigatingthenet/tp/How-to-Properly-Research-Online.htm.

MacDonald, W. Brock, and June Seel. "Research Using the Internet." *University of Toronto Library*. Accessed May 29, 2014 from http://www.writing.utoronto.ca/advice/reading-and-researching/research-using-internet.

Schneider, Fritz, Nancy Blachman, and Eric Fredricksen. *How to Do Everything with Google*. Emeryville, CA: McGraw-Hill Osborne, 2012.

INDEX

ABOUT THE AUTHOR

Kezia Endsley is an editor and author from Indianapolis, Indiana. She has been involved in the technical publishing field since the days of CompuServe, before the "real" Internet took off. She has enjoyed being a part of educating people of all ages about technical subjects for over two decades. In addition to editing technical publications and writing books for teens, she enjoys running and triathlons, reading, and spending time with her family.